Hart Hill Nursery School
Whitecroft Road
Luton
Beds
LU2 0JS
01582 731701

My Body, Your Body

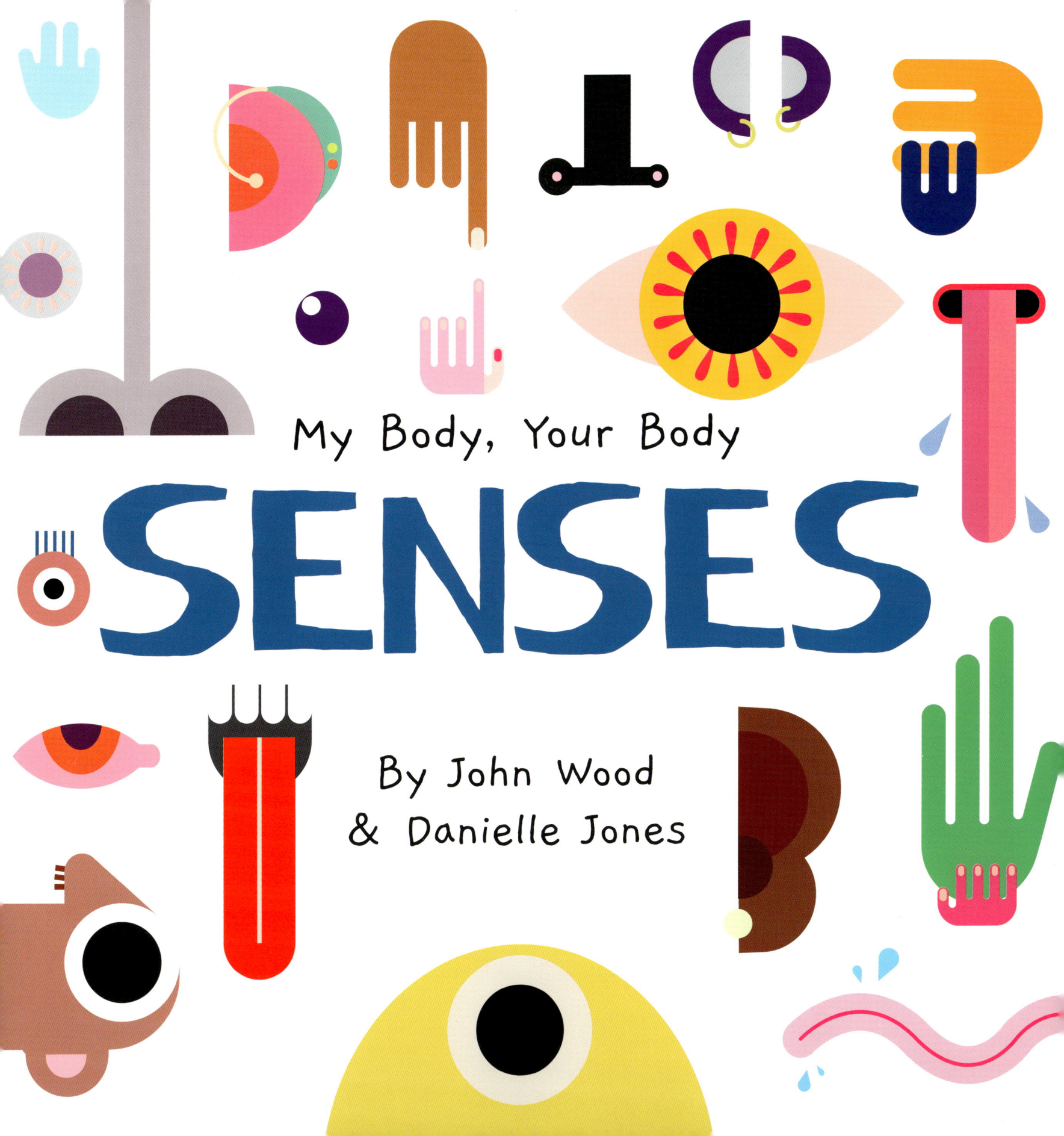

SENSES

By John Wood
& Danielle Jones

BookLife
PUBLISHING

©2019
BookLife Publishing Ltd.
King's Lynn, Norfolk PE30 4LS

All rights reserved. Printed in Malaysia.
A catalogue record for this book is available
from the British Library.

ISBN: 978-1-78637-745-6

Written by: John Wood

Edited by: Madeline Tyler

Designed by: Danielle Jones

*All facts, statistics, web addresses and URLs
in this book were verified as valid and
accurate at time of writing. No responsibility
for any changes to external websites
or references can be accepted by either
the author or publisher.*

All images are courtesy of danjazzia
via Shutterstock.com, unless otherwise
specified. With thanks to Getty Images,
Thinkstock Photo and iStockphoto.
Additional illustrations by Danielle Jones.

I have senses.

You have senses.

But what are senses?

3

Skin lets you **FEEL** things.

Is this HOT or COLD?

Too HARD, too soft, or too spiky to hold?

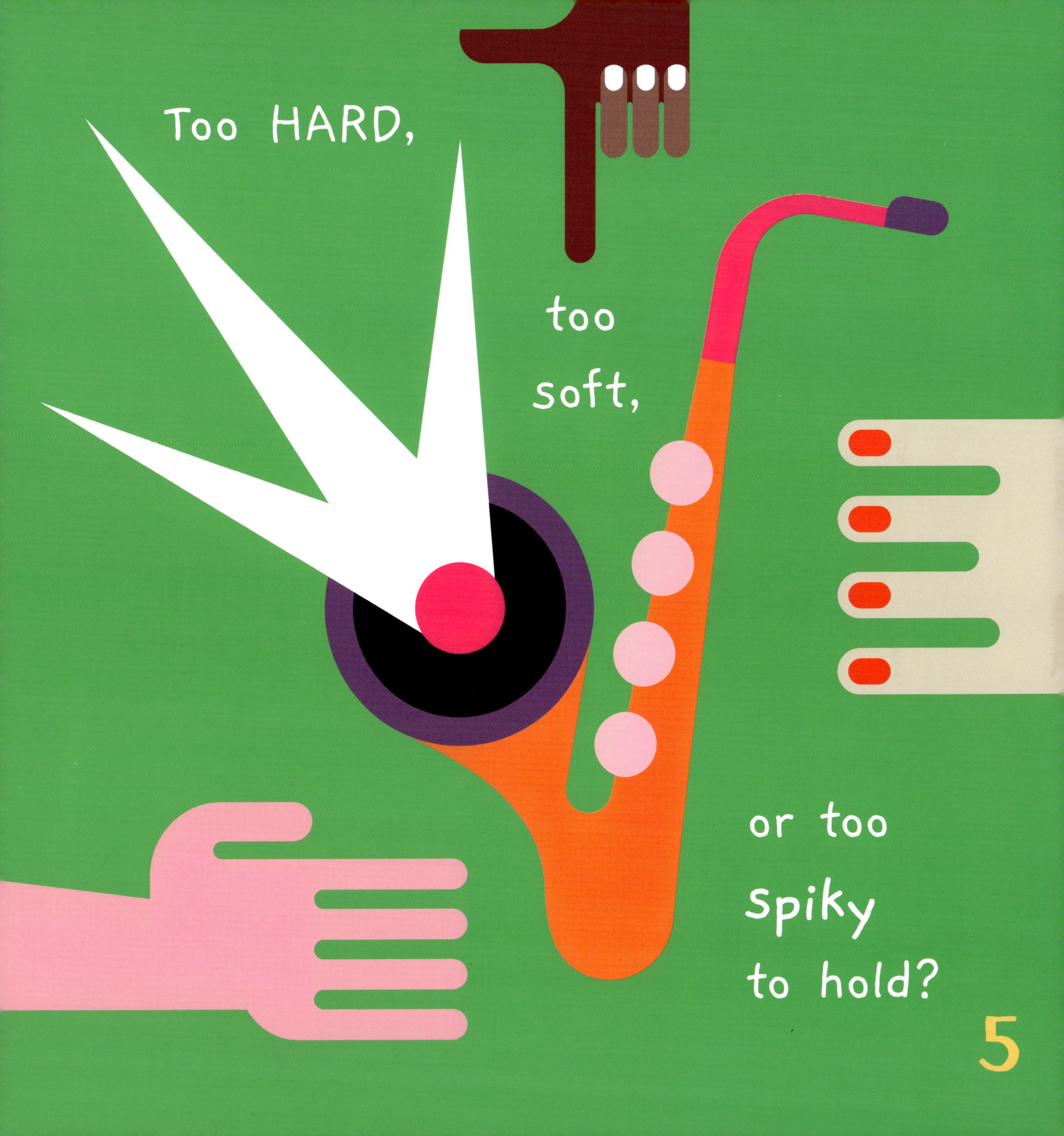

Ears let you HEAR. Can you hear different sounds?

Quiet or LOUD, there are sounds all around.

Some people's ears cannot hear very well.

They wear a hearing aid.

No need to
YELL!

Eyes let us SEE. Can you see all the sights?

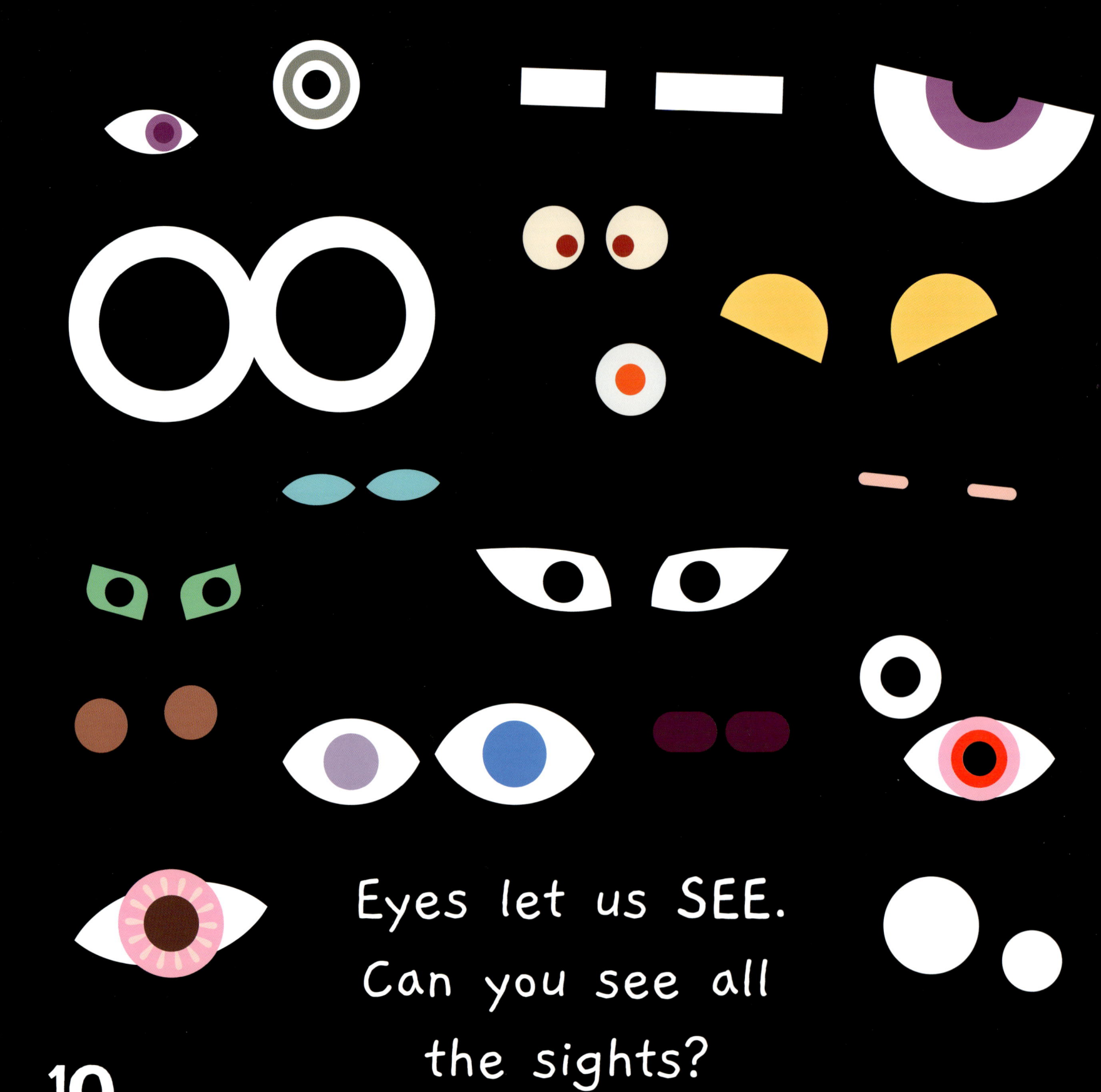

10

People and buildings
and pictures
and lights?

11

You might need GLASSES to read every word.

12

Glasses can help us a lot, I have heard.

Some of us cannot see much with our eyes.

We can use guide dogs or sticks to get by.

Noses can let us **SMELL** all of the smells.

Animals, flowers –

and dinner as well!

He cannot smell
with a nose FULL of SNOT.

Some people cannot smell, no matter what.

Tongues let us TASTE all the things that we eat.

Ice cream and carrots
and sugary sweets!

21

Your sense of BALANCE keeps you off the floor.

You might still fall,
then your bum would be **sore**.

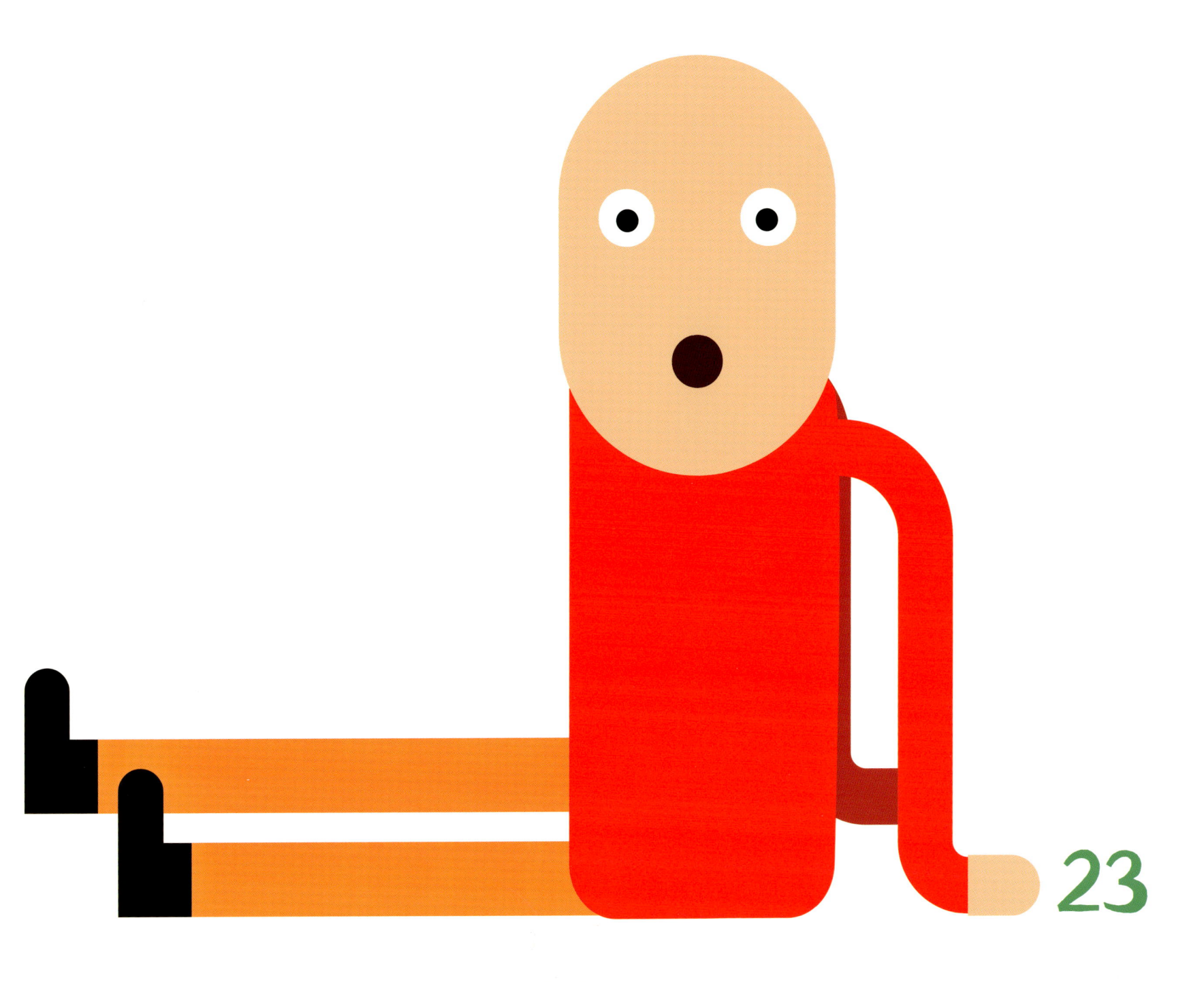

We would go on.
Oh, if only we could!
Senses are **different** and **lovely**
and **good**.